Help Yourself in

READING QUR'ÂN

2nd Edition: September 2004

© **Maktaba Dar-us-Salam, 1995**

King Fahd National Library Cataloging-in-Publication Data

Abdus Salam, Qari

Help Yourself in reading qur'ân-Riyadh.

64p., 17x24 cm. **ISBN 9960-740-49-8**

I-Islam-General principles II-Title

418.24 dc. 3684/15

Legal Deposit no. 3684/15

ISBN 9960-740-49-8

HEAD OFFICE

P.O. Box: 22743, Riyadh 11416 K.S.A.Tel: 00966-01-4033962/4043432 Fax: 4021659

E-mail: riyadh@dar-us-salam.com, darussalam@awalnet.net.sa Website: www.dar-us-salam.com

K.S.A. Darussalam Showrooms:

Riyadh

Olaya branch: Tel 00966-1-4614483 Fax: 4644945

Malaz branch: Tel 4735220 Fax: 4735221

- **Jeddah**
  Tel: 00966-2-6879254 Fax: 6336270
  Madinah
  Tel: 00966-4-815-1121 Fax: 815 1121
- **Al-Khobar**
  Tel: 00966-3-8692900 Fax: 00966-3-8691551

U.A.E

- **Darussalam, Sharjah U.A.E**
  Tel: 00971-6-5632623 Fax: 5632624
  Sharjah@dar-us-salam.com

PAKISTAN

- **Darussalam,** 36 B Lower Mall, Lahore
  Tel: 0092-42-724 0024 Fax: 7354072
  Lahore@dar-us-salam.com
- **Rahman Market, Ghazni Street**
  Urdu Bazar Lahore
  Tel: 0092-42-7120054 Fax: 7320703

U.S.A

- **Darussalam, Houston**
  P.O Box: 79194 Tx 77279
  Tel: 001-713-722 0419 Fax: 001-713-722 0431
  E-mail: sales@dar-us-salam. Com.
- **Darussalam, New York** 186 Atlantic Ave, Brooklyn
  New York-11217, Tel: 001-718-625 5925
  Fax: 718-625 1511
  Email: newyork@dar-us-salam.com.

U.K

- **Darussalam International Publications Ltd.**
  Leyton Business Centre
  Unit – 17, Etloe Road, Leyton, London, E10 7BT
  Tel: 00 44 20 8539 4885 Fax: 00 44 20 8539 4889
  Mobile: 00 44 7947 306 706
- **Darussalam International Publications Limited**
  146 Park Road,
  London NW8 7RG Tel: 00 44 20 725 2246
- **Darussalam**
  398-400 Coventry Road, Small Heath
  Birmingham, B10 0UF
  Tel: 0121 77204792 Fax: 0121 772 4345
  E-mail: info@darussalamuk.com
  Web: www.darussalamuk.com

HONG KONG

- **Peacetech**
  A2, 4/F Tsim Sha Tsui Mansion
  83-87 Nathan Road Tsimsbatsui
  Kowloon, Hong Kong
  Tel: 00852 2369 2722 Fax: 00852 2369 2944
  Mobile: 00852 97123624

MALAYSIA

- **Darussalam International Publications Ltd.**
  No.109 A Jalan SS 21/A, Damansara Utama
  47400, Petaling Jaya, Selangor, Malaysia
  Tel: 00603 7710 9750 Fax: 603 7710 0749

FRANCE

- Editions & Librairie Essalam
  135, Bd de Ménilmontant- 75011 Paris
  Tél: 0033-01- 43 38 19 56/ 44 83
  Fax: 0033-01- 43 57 44 31
  E-mail: essalam@wanadoo.FR

AUSTRALIA

- ICIS: Ground Floor 165-171, Haldon St.
  Lakemba NSW 2195, Australia
  Tel: 00612 9758 4040 Fax: 9758 4030

SINGAPORE

- Muslim Converts Association of Singapore
  32 Onan Road The Galaxy Singapore- 424484
  Tel: 0065-440 6924, 348 8344
  Fax: 440 6724

SRI LANKA

- Darul Kitab 6, Nimal Road, Colombo-4
  Tel: 0094-1-589 038 Fax: 0094-74 722433

KUWAIT

- Islam Presentation Committee
  Enlightenment Book Shop
  P.O. Box: 1613, Safat 13017 Kuwait
  Tel: 00965-244 7526, Fax: 240 0057

SOUTH AFRICA

- Islamic Da`wah Movement (IDM)
  48009 Qualbert 4078 Durban,South Africa
  Tel: 0027-31-304-6883
  Fax: 0027-31-305-1292
  E-mail: idm@ion.co.za

كَيْفَ تَتْلُو الْقُرْآن

Help Yourself in READING QUR'ÂN

Compiled by
Qari Abdussalam

DARUSSALAM
GLOBAL LEADER IN ISLAMIC BOOKS
Riyadh · Jeddah · Al-Khobar · Sharjah
Lahore · London · Houston · New York

بسم الله الرحمن الرحيم

In the Name of Allâh
the Most Beneficent
the Most Merciful

PUBLISHER`S NOTE

The reading of Qur`ân is of prime importance to a Muslim. Qur`ân was revealed in Arabic language and it should also be read in Arabic only, because the actual meaning of Qur`ân in Arabic can not be expressed in the translation of any language. That is why, it is an established fact that the reading of any translation of Qur`ân does not mean that the actual Qur`ân has been read.

It is the basic teaching of Islam to read Qur`ân as many times as one can. The reward of the recitation of Qur`ân and remembrance of Allah is very great, and we can get that reward only if we are able to read the Qur`ân in its original language Arabic.

But the Muslims, who can not read Arabic, are unable to get benefited by reading the Qur`ân in its language. To ease them from this difficulty, we expressed our desire to Qari Abdus Salam to prepare some kind of helping guide, we are happy to express that Qari Abdus Salam prepared this book taking keen interest and using all his expertise of teaching Arabic language and Qur`ân. May Allâh favour him with His Mercy.

In this book, through transliteration, an easy approach has been offered to learn reading Arabic in a simple way. Through step by step lessons, all the necessary points are such explained that one can easily understand and read Arabic to earn the ability of reciting Qur`ân with its correct pronunciation. Hence this book is as useful for children as it is for elder people.

As no such attempt was made before, which can help people learning to read Arabic and recite Qur`ân, we hope that all persons, who were unable to read Arabic, will appreciate our efforts and get the advantage.

We hope that Allâh will make our efforts successful and bless all of us abundantly– *Amin.*

Abdul Malik Mujahid

General Manager

Lesson 1

The Arabic Alphabet

Qaaf	ق	Zaa	ز	Alif	ا
Kaaf	ك	Seen	س	Baa	ب
Laam	ل	Sheen	ش	Taa	ت
Meem	م	ص Ṣaad	ص	Thaa	ث
Noon	ن	ض Ḍaad	ض	Jeem	ج
Waaw	و	ط Ṭaa	ط	ح Ḥaa	ح
Haa	هـ	ظ Ẓaa	ظ	Khaa	خ
Hamzah	ء	ع Aieen	ع	Daal	د
Yaa	ي	غ Ghaieen	غ	ذ Dhaal	ذ
Yaa	ے	Faa	ف	Raa	ر

Exercise 1

هـ	ر	و	ب
ق	ش	ص	ج
م	ي	ن	د
ح	ع	ء	س
ظ	ذ	ف	ز
ث	ض	ل	ط
ي	ا	خ	ك
	ت		غ

Lesson 2

Vowels

There are six vowels in Arabic Alphabet, three of them are short and the other three are long.

Short Vowels

(i) Vowel “a” (a= َـ*Fatḥah*) (Ja= جَ) (Ba= بَ)

This mark (َـ) written on the top of the Arabic letter is called *Fatḥah* and stands for short (a) this vowel is pronounced as “a” in the “apple”.

(1) (*Fatḥah* َـ)

Sha	شَ	Kha	خَ	ء Aa	أَ
ص Ṣa	صَ	Da	دَ	Ba	بَ
ض Ḍa	ضَ	ذ Dha	ذَ	Ta	تَ
ط Ṭa	طَ	Ra	رَ	Tha	ثَ
ظ Ẓa	ظَ	Za	زَ	Ja	جَ
ع Aa	عَ	Sa	سَ	ح Ḥa	حَ

Ha	هَـ ـهَ ـهَـ هَ	La	لَ	<u>Gh</u>a	غَ
Åa	ءَ	Ma	مَ	Fa	فَ
Ya	يَ	Na	نَ	Qa	قَ
Ya	ےَ	Wa	وَ	Ka	كَ

Note:

The Arabic letters with vowels may be learnt by spellings as:

(Ba = بَ) **Baa** *Fatḥah* **<u>Ba</u>**

(Ja = جَ) **Jeem** *Fatḥah* **<u>Ja</u>**

(Da = دَ) **Daal** *Fatḥah* **<u>Da</u>**

Until you do not learn the previous lesson do not begin the next one.

(ii) Vowel "i" (i ـِ *Kasrah*)

(Ji = جِ) (Bi = بِ)

This mark (ـِ) written below the Arabic letter is called *Kasrah* which stands for short "i". This "i" is pronounced as the vowel in "tin".

(2) (*Kasrah* ـِ)

ض Ḍi	ضِ	Di	دِ	Íe	إِ
ط Ṭi	طِ	ذ Dhi	ذِ	Bi	بِ
ظ Ẓi	ظِ	Ri	رِ	Ti	تِ
ع Ie	عِ	Zi	زِ	Thi	ثِ
Ghi	غِ	Si	سِ	Ji	جِ
Fi	فِ	Shi	شِ	ح Ḥi	حِ
Qi	قِ	ص Ṣi	صِ	Khi	خِ

Íe	ءِ	Ni	نِ	Ki	كِ
Ye	يِ	Wi	وِ	Li	لِ
Ye	ےِ	Hi	هِـ = هِ	Mi	مِ

Note:

These alphabets may be pronounced in this way:

(Bi = بِ) **Baa** *Kasrah* **Bi**

(Ji = جِ) **Jeem** *Kasrah* **Ji**

(Di = دِ) **Daal** *Kasrah* **Di**

(iii) Vowel "u" (u ـُ ḍammah)

(Ju = جُ) (Bu = بُ)

This mark (ـُ) on the Arabic letter stands for short "u". This "u" is pronounced like the vowel in "pull".
This mark (ـُ) is called in Arabic *ḍammah*.

(3) (*ḍammah* ـُ)

ظ Ẓu	ظُ	ذ Dhu	ذُ	ء Úu	أُ
ع Uu	عُ	Ru	رُ	Bu	بُ
Ghu	غُ	Zu	زُ	Tu	تُ
Fu	فُ	Su	سُ	Thu	ثُ
Qu	قُ	Shu	شُ	Ju	جُ
Ku	كُ	ص Ṣu	صُ	ح Ḥu	حُ
Lu	لُ	ض Ḍu	ضُ	Khu	خُ
Mu	مُ	ط Ṭu	طُ	Du	دُ

Yu	يُ	Hu	هُـ	Nu	نُ
Yu	ـئُ	Ủu	ءُ	Wu	وُ

Note:

You may spell these letters in this way:

(Bu = بُ) Baa *Ḍammah* Bu

(Ju = جُ) Jeem *Ḍammah* Ju

(Du = دُ) Daal *Ḍammah* Du

Exercise 2

(Read and Spell)

مُ	كِ	سُ	بِ	دَ
زُ	لِ	فَ	ءُ	جِ
شُ	تِ	هِـ	غِ	يُ
حُ	ذِ	ظَ	رِ = ـرِ	قَ
طَ	أَ	صُ	نَ	ثِ
مِ	ضَ	عُ	خِ	وُ

Lesson 3

Absence of Vowel (*Sukoon* ـْ أَبْ)

(Jab = جَبْ) (Min = مِنْ)

This circle (ـْ) above the letter is called *Sukoon*. It indicates that such a letter is not followed by any vowel sound, but the alphabet with *Sukoon* is joined with the former alphabet.

(4) (*Sukoon* ـْ)

Ȧṭ	أَطْ	Ȧd	أَدْ	Ȧb	أَبْ
Iṭ	إِطْ	Id	إِدْ	Ib	إِبْ
Uṭ	أُطْ	Ud	أُدْ	Ub	أُبْ
Ȧgh	أَغْ	Ȧs	أَسْ	Ȧj	أَجْ
Igh	إِغْ	Is	إِسْ	Ij	إِجْ
Ugh	أُغْ	Us	أُسْ	Uj	أُجْ

Din̊	دِنْ	Ím̊	إِمْ	Áf	أَفْ
Dur̊	دُرْ	Ún̊	أُنْ	Íq	إِقْ
Qul̊	قُلْ	Jan̊	جَنْ	Úk̊	أُكْ
Hum̊	هُـمْ	Jin̊	جِنْ	Ál̊	أَلْ

Note :

You may spell this lesson in this way:

(Áb̊ = أَبْ) Hamzah *Fatḥah* Baa *Sākin* <u>Áb</u>

(Íb̊ = إِبْ) Hamzah *Kasrah* Baa *Sākin* <u>Íb</u>

(Úb = أُبْ) Hamzah *Ḍammah* Baa *Sākin* <u>Úb</u>

(Jin = جِنْ) Jeem *Kasrah* Noon *Sākin* <u>Jin̊</u>

Exercise 3

أَبْ	أُسْ	أُفْ	إِحْ	أَوْ
إِبْ	أَطْ	أَشْ	أُحْ	إِوْ
أُبْ	إِطْ	إِشْ	أَزْ	أُوْ
أَجْ	أُطْ	أُشْ	إِزْ	أَتْ
إِجْ	إِغْ	أَقْ	أُزْ	إِتْ
أُجْ	أُكْ	إِقْ	أَعْ	أُتْ
أَدْ	إِمْ	أُقْ	إِعْ	أَثْ
إِدْ	إِنْ	أَرْ	أُعْ	إِثْ
أُدْ	أُنْ	إِرْ	أَصْ	أُثْ
أَسْ	أَفْ	أُرْ	إِصْ	أَيْ
إِسْ	إِفْ	أَحْ	أُصْ	إِيْ

Lesson 4

Long Vowels

(i) Vowel (ā = ا — Alif *Maddah*)
(Jā = جَ ا) (Bā = بَ ا)

If the letter Alif (ا) comes after an alphabet with *Fatḥah* (ـَ), then this Alif will be pronounced like double *Fatḥah* and this "ā" is pronounced like "a" of "father".

Joint / unjoint		Joint / unjoint	
Aā	عَ ا = عَا	Dā	دَ ا = دَا
Tā	تَ ا = تَا	Rā	رَ ا = رَا
Fā	فَ ا = فَا	Bā	بَ ا = بَا
Kā	كَ ا = كَا	Jā	جَ ا = جَا
Lā	لَ ا = لَا	Sā	سَ ا = سَا
Mā	مَ ا = مَا	Ṣā	صَ ا = صَا
Nā	نَ ا = نَا	Ṭā	طَ ا = طَا
Qā	قَ ا = قَا	Hā	هَ ا = هَا

(ii) Long Vowel (ū = وْ Waaw *Maddah*)
(Jū = جُ وْ) (Bū = بُ وْ)

If the letter Waaw (ـوْ) with *Sukoon*(ـْـ) comes after an alphabet with *Ḍammah* (ـُـ), then this Waaw which is called Waaw *Maddah* will be pronounced like double *Ḍammah* "ū" and this "ū" is pronounced like the vowel of "food".

Joint / unjoint		Joint / unjoint	
Mū	مُ وْ = مُوْ	Bū	بُ وْ = بُـوْ
Nū	نُ وْ = نُوْ	Jū	جُ وْ = جُـوْ
Hū	هُـ وْ = هُوْ	ص Ṣū	صُ وْ = صُوْ
Yū	يُ وْ = يُـوْ	ط Ṭū	طُ وْ = طُـوْ
Dū	دُ وْ = دُوْ	ع Uū	عُ وْ = عُـوْ
Zū	زُوْ = زُوْ	Fū	فُ وْ = فُـوْ
Sū	سُ وْ = سُـوْ	Kū	كُ وْ = كُـوْ
Tū	تُ وْ = تُوْ	Lū	لُ وْ = لُـوْ

(iii) Long Vowel (ī = يْ Yaa *Maddah*)

(Jī = جِ يْ) (Bī = بِ يْ)

If the letter Yaa with *Sukoon* (ـْـ) comes after an alphabet with *Kasrah* (ـِـ), then this *Yaa Maddah* will be pronounced like double vowel *Kasrah* (ـِـ) = "ī" and this "ī" is pronounced like the vowel of "deep".

Joint / unjoint			Joint / unjoint		
Lī	لِيْ	لِ يْ =	Bī	بِيْ	بِ يْ =
Mī	مِيْ	مِ يْ =	Jī	جِيْ	جِ يْ =
Nī	نِيْ	نِ يْ =	Shī	شِيْ	شِ يْ =
Hī	هِيْ	هِـ يْ =	Ṭī	طِيْ	طِ يْ =
Yī	يِـيْ	يِ يْ =	Eī	عِيْ	عِ يْ =
Sī	سِيْ	سِ يْ =	Fī	فِيْ	فِ يْ =
Dī	دِيْ	دِ يْ =	Kī	كِيْ	كِ يْ =
Zī	زِيْ	زِ يْ =	Ṣī	صِيْ	صِ يْ =

Exercise 4

(Revision)

Mixed	Yaa *Maddah*	Waaw *Maddah*	Alif *Maddah*
جَا	بِ يْ = بِيْ	بُ وْ = بُوْ	دَ ا = دَا
صُوْ	جِ يْ = جِيْ	جُ وْ = جُوْ	رَ ا = رَا
طِيْ	شِ يْ = شِيْ	صُ وْ = صُوْ	بَ ا = بَا
عَـا	طِ يْ = طِيْ	طُ وْ = طُوْ	جَ ا = جَـا
مُـوْ	عِ يْ = عِيْ	عُ وْ = عُوْ	سَ ا = سَا
نِـيْ	فِ يْ = فِيْ	فُ وْ = فُوْ	صَ ا = صَا
دَا	كِ يْ = كِيْ	كُ وْ = كُوْ	طَ ا = طَـا
بُـوْ	لِ يْ = لِيْ	لُ وْ = لُوْ	عَ ا = عَـا
جِـيْ	مِ يْ = مِيْ	مُ وْ = مُوْ	فَ ا = فَـا
سَـا	نِ يْ = نِيْ	هُـ وْ = هُوْ	كَ ا = كَا
سِـيْ	هِـ يْ = هِيْ	يُ وْ = يُوْ	لَ ا = لَا
سُـوْ	يِ يْ = يِـيْ	حُ وْ = حُـوْ	مَ ا = مَـا

Lesson 5

(i) Different joint shapes of *Compounds Words.*

	2		1
Baa Haa Raa	بهر	Laam Alif	لا
Aieen Aieen	عع	Laam Jeem	لج
Aieen Noon Haa	عنه	Kaaf Laam	كل
Laam Haa	له	Baa Laam Baa	بلب
Laam Yaa Haa	ليه	Kaaf Alif	كا
Khaa Dhaal Taa	خذة	Taa Kaaf Thaa	تكث
Taa Meem Taa	تمت	Thaa Meem Yaa	ثمي
Yaa Ḥaa	يح	Qaaf Ḍaad Yaa	قضي
Seen Hamzah Laam	سئل	Yaa Thaa Noon	يثن
Taa Ḥaa Taa	تحت	Thaa Baa Laam	ثبل
Baa Aieen Daal	بعد	Baa Laam Daal	بلد
Yaa Seen	يٰس	Yaa Faa Raa	يفر
Taa Gheen Dhal	تغذ	Noon Ṣaad	نص

(ii) Compound Words with *Short Vowel*
(*Fatḥah* ـَ = a)
(Read the syllables and then the word)

2		1	
Sa La Ma	سَ لَ مَ	Åa Ba	أَ بَ
Ra Za Qa	رَزَقَ	Da Ma	دَ مَ
Ba Da Na	بَـدَنَ	Ra Sa	رَ سَ
Da Ra Sa	دَرَسَ	Wa La	وَ لَ
Wa Ra <u>Th</u>a	وَرَثَ	Ṣa Fa	صَفَ
Åa Ma La	عَـمَلَ	Ba Sa	بَـسَ
Ḍa Ra Ba	ضَرَبَ	Ya Da	يَـدَ
Ma Ra Ḍa	مَرَضَ	Ja Ra	جَرَ
Ha La Ka	هَلَكَ	Ka Ta	كَتَ
<u>Dh</u>a Ka Ra	ذَكَرَ	Ma Åa	مَعَ
Ra Fa Åa	رَفَعَ	La Ka	لَكَ
Sa La Ma	سَلَمَ	Ta Na	تَنَ

(iii) Compound Words with *Short Vowel*

(*Kasrah* ـِ = i)

	2		1
Yi Hi	يِـهِ	ءIe Bi	إِ بِ
ءIe Bi Li	إِبِـلِ	Di Mi	دِ مِ
Fi Li Mi	فِلِـمِ	Ri Si	رِ سِ
Ri Zi Qi	رِزِقِ	Wi Li	وِ لِ
Si Ri Fi	سِـرِفِ	عIe طṬi	عِـطِ
عIe Mi Di	عِـمِـدِ	Mi Li	مِـلِ
Mi Li Ki	مِـلِـكِ	Si Ri	سِـرِ
Fi عIe Li	فِـعِلِ	Fi Ki	فِـكِ
Qi Di Ri	قِـدِرِ	Bi Ni	بِـنِ
ذ<u>Dhi</u> Hi Ni	ذِهِـنِ	Bi Ki	بِـكِ
Ji Ri Bi	جِرِبِ	Ji Bi	جِـبِ

(IV) Compound Words with *Short Vowel*

(*Ḍammah* = ـُ = u)

2		1	
Du Ru Su	دُ رُسُ	ء Uu Bu	أُبُ
Mu Ru Du	مُرُدُ	Du Mu	دُمُ
Ju Ru Fu	جُرُفُ	Ru Su	رُسُ
ع Uu Lu Mu	عُلُمُ	Wu Lu	وُلُ
ص Ṣu ح Ḥu Fu	صُحُفُ	Du ع Uu	دُعُ
Ru Su Lu	رُسُلُ	Ju Fu	جُفُ
Shu Khu ذ Dhu	شُخُذُ	Ku Lu	كُلُ
Ku Tu Bu	كُتُبُ	Shu Khu	شُخُ
ع Uu Nu Qu	عُنُقُ	Nu Su	نُسُ
Mu Ru ض Ḍu	مُ رُضُ	Hu Shu	هُشُ
Mu Ru ض Ḍu	مُرُضُ	ح Ḥu ض Ḍu	حُضُ
Su Ru Ru	سُرُرُ	ع Uu Qu	عُقُ

Exercise 5

وُ لُ	فِـكِ	بَـدَنَ	أَ بَ
دُ عُ	يِـهِ	دَ رَسَ	دَ مَ
خُـفُ	جِـبِ	ضَرَبَ	رَ سَ
كُـلُ	إِبِـلِ	مَرَضَ	وَ لَ
شُخُ	فِلِـمِ	إِ بِ	صَفَ
هُشُ	رِزِقِ	دِ مِ	بَـسَ
عُـقُ	مِلِكِ	رِ سِ	تَنَ
دُ رُسُ	قِـدِرِ	وِ لِ	كَتَ
جُرُفُ	أُبُ	عِطِ	مَعَ
صُحُفُ	دُ مُ	مِـلِ	لَـكَ
رُسُـلُ	رُ سُ	سِـرِ	سَـلَمَ
كُـتُبُ	سُـرُفُ	وِزِنِ	جَرَبَ

Lesson 6

Revision		Miscellaneous	
Åb	أَبْ	Åa Na	أَنَ
Min	مِنْ	Hu Wa	هُوَ
Hud	هُدْ	Li Ya	لِيَ
ع Aa Ra Sha	عَرَشَ	Ta Ku	تَكُ
Lil	لِلْ	Ůu Mi La	أُمِلَ
Nu Ṣi Ra	نُصِرَ	La Ṭu Fa	لَطُفَ
ع Il Mu	عِلْمُ	Khu Li Qa	خُلِقَ
Las Ta	لَسْتَ	Qa La Mi	قَلَمِ
Kun Tu	كُنْتُ	Ra Bi Ḥa	رَبِحَ
Naḥ Nu	نَحْنُ	Sa Mi ع Aa	سَمِعَ
Mul Ki	مُلْكِ	Fi Ka Ri	فِكَرِ

Alif (Hamzah) with *Sukoon* (ـأْ)

(Jaå=جَاْ) (Baå =بَـاْ)

Raå Sa	رَأْسَ	Taå	تَـأْ
Kaå Sa	كَـأْسَ	Raå	رَأْ
Faå Ti	فَـأْتِ	Saå	سَـأْ
Shaå Nu	شَـأْنُ	Maå	مَـأْ

Some more Words

Idha Ḥasada	إِذَا حَسَدَ	Ta Qī	تَقِـيْ
Lam Yalid	لَـمْ يَلِـدْ	Qī La	قِيْلَ
Wa Lam Yūlad	وَلَـمْ يُوْلَـدْ	Fī Hi	فِـيْهِ
Åa Bu Du	أَعْبُـدُ	Åa Jab	عَجَبْ
Na Bu Du	نَعْبُـدُ	Ka Ram	كَـرَمْ
Ån Åm Ta	أَنْعَـمْتَ	Yu Ka Dh	يُكَـذْ
Ånta	أَنْـتَ	La Hum	لَـهُمْ

Words of "*Leen*" Waaw —Yaa

(Khay =خَيْ) (Khaw =خَوْ)

Ảy Na	أَيْنَ	Ảw	أَوْ
Law Ḥi (ح)	لَوْحِ	Ảy	أَيْ
Khay Ra	خَيْـرَ	Daw	دَوْ
Khaw Fu	خَـوْفُ	Day	دَيْ
Bay Ti	بَيْتِ	Jaw	جَــوْ
Qaw Su	قَوْسُ	Jay	جَــيْ
(ع) Ảy Ni	عَيْـنِ	Shaw	شَــوْ
Yaw Ma	يَـوْمَ	Shay	شَــيْ
(ح) Ḥaw (ض) Ḍu	حَـوْضُ	Law	لَــوْ
Kay Fa	كَيْفَ	Lay	لَــيْ
Khay La	خَيْلَ	Haw	هَــوْ
Lay Li	لَيْلِ	Hay	هَــيْ

Exercise 6

أَنَ	مِنْ	شَأْنُ	دَيْ
هُوَ	عَرَش	أَبَا	جَوْ
لِيَ	نُصِرَ	عُلاَ	جَيْ
تَكُ	نَحْنُ	زَادَ	شَوْ
أُمِلَ	تَأْ	نُوْحُ	شَيْ
لَطُفَ	رَأْ	لَفِيْ	أَيْنَ
خُلِقَ	سَأْ	كَرَمْ	خَيْرَ
قَلَمِ	مَأْ	إِذَا حَسَدَ	خَوْفُ
رَبِحَ	رَأْسَ	أَوْ	بَيْتِ
بَدَنَ	كَأْسَ	أَيْ	أَلَمْ تَرَ
سَمِعَ	فَأْتِ	دَوْ	كَيْفَ فَعَلَ

Lesson 7

Compound Words with four alphabets

Ya <u>Kh</u>ā fu	يَخَافُ	Ṭa li bu	طَالِبُ
Ma aa kum	مَعَكُمْ	Aā di li	عَادِلِ
Us kun	اُسْكُنْ	A<u>kh</u> ra ja	أَخْرَجَ
Ra ḥee mi	رَحِيْمِ	Aa bu du	أَعْبُدُ
Qu ri aa	قُرِئَ	Kaw <u>th</u>a ra	كَوْثَرَ
Yal aa bu	يَلْعَبُ	Yur si la	يُرْسِلَ
Aa ri ḍ	أَعْرِضْ	Yu<u>gh</u> nī	يُغْنِيْ
Alam na<u>sh</u> raḥ		أَلَمْ نَشْرَحْ	
Laka ṣad ra ka		لَكَ صَدْرَكَ	
Wa i<u>dh</u>ā qeela la hum		وَإِذَا قِيْلَ لَهُمْ	
Wa mā ka sa ba		وَمَا كَسَبَ	

Exercise 7

طَالِبُ	كَوْثَرَ	مَعَكُمْ	يَلْعَبُ
عَادِلِ	يُرْسِلَ	أُسْكُنْ	أَعْرِضْ
أَخْرَجَ	يُغْنِيْ	رَحِيْمِ	يَهْدِيْ
أَعْبُدُ	يَخَافُ	قُرِئَ	تَجْدِيْ

أَلَمْ نَشْرَحْ لَكَ صَدْرَكَ

وَإِذَا قِيْلَ لَهُمْ

وَمَا كَسَبَ

أَفَلَا يَعْلَمُ إِذَا بُعْثِرَ

وَجَعَلْنَا نَوْمَكُمْ سُبَاتَا

وَقَالَ الْإِنْسَانُ مَالَهَا

Lesson 8

(*Tanween* ـٌ ـٍ ـً تنوین)

Tanween **means two times short vowels on the alphabet which sounds like Noon "نون" with *Sukoon***

Tin = Tin	ةٍ = تِنْ	Ản = Ản	أً = أَنْ
Tun = Tun	ةٌ = تُنْ	Ban = Ban	بً = بَنْ
Man = Man	مًا = مَنْ	Jan = Jan	جً = جَنْ
Min = Min	مٍ = مِنْ	Ỉn = Ỉn	إٍ = إِنْ
Mun = Mun	مٌ = مُنْ	Bin = Bin	بٍ = بِنْ
Ran = Ran	رًا = رَنْ	Jin = Jin	جٍ = جِنْ
Wan = Wan	وًا = وَنْ	Ủn = Ủn	أٌ = أُنْ
<u>Dh</u>an = <u>Dh</u>an	ذًى = ذَنْ	Bun = Bun	بٌ = بُنْ
Kan	كًا	Jun = Jun	جٌ = جُنْ
Ran	رًى	Tan = Tan	ةً = تَنْ

Qad Rin	قَدْرٍ	Fan	فًــى
Naf Sin	نَفْسٍ	Bad Rin	بَدْرٍ

Some more Words

ع Aa lee mun	عَلِيْمٌ	ض ع Baa ḍin	بَعْضٍ
Ả ma ran	أَمَرًا	Shaả nin	شَأْنٍ
ع Ina ban	عِنَبًا	Shay ỉn	شَيْءٍ
Riz qan	رِزْقًا	ص Na ṣi rin	نَاصِرٍ
ذ ع Dhar an	ذَرْعًا	Ki lā bin	كِلَابٍ
ع Us ran	عُسْرًا	Dā run	دَارٌ
Ya dan	يَدًا	ض Ḍa ra bun	ضَرَبٌ
Hu dan	هُدًى	Sh am sun	شَمْسٌ
Qud ra tan	قُدْرَةً	Qa ma run	قَمَرٌ
ص Ṣa da qa tan	صَدَقَةً	ع Um yun	عُمْيٌ

ع Il min	عِلْمٍ	Ba si ط ṭun	بَاسِطٌ
Sha kū run	شَكُوْرٌ	Sa mee ع un	سَمِيْعٌ
Qu ray Shin	قُرَيْشٍ	Nu su kin	نُسُكٍ
ص Ṣin wā nun	صِنْوَانٌ	Jah ra tan	جَهْرَةً
Bun yā nun	بُنْيَانٌ	Ra ůoo fun	رَءُوْفٌ

Miscellaneous

Bay na kum	بَيْنَكُمْ	Ån ta	أَنْتَ
Tab ta ghī	تَبْتَغِيْ	Ån ع aam ta	أَنْعَمْتَ
Ghi shā wa tun	غِشَاوَةٌ	Min hum	مِنْهُمْ
Al ح ḥam du	اَلْحَمْدُ	Min Åaja lin	مِنْ أَجَلٍ
Nū ح ḥee hi	نُوْحِيْهِ	Åع a la mu	أَعْلَمُ
Faw qa ha	فَوْقَهَا	ع In da	عِنْدَ
ع Aa lay him	عَلَيْهِمْ	Ån sha ra	أَنْشَرَ

ح Taḥ yaw na	تَحْيَوْنَ	Ủn zi la	أُنْزِلَ
Taả wee lu	تَأْوِيْلُ	Ản fu sa	أَنْفُسَ
Biả run	بِئْرٌ	Ya tee man	يَتِيْمًا
Yus ran	يُسْرًا	Yan qa li bu	يَنْقَلِبُ
ع Ii na ban	عِنَبًا	Fa raq na	فَرَقْنَا
Min <u>kh</u>aw fin	مِنْ خَوْفٍ		
Ru ủoo su ka	رُءُوْسُكَ		
Mā tub doo na	مَا تُبْدُوْنَ		
ع Aay nun jā riya tun	عَيْنٌ جَارِيَةٌ		
ذ Dhā maq ra ba tin	ذَا مَقْرَبَةٍ		
Nā run ح ḥā miya tun	نَارٌ حَامِيَةٌ		

Exercise 8

أً = أَنْ	مًا=مَنْ	ضَرَبٌ	صَدَقَةً
بً=بَنْ	مٍ=مِنْ	شَمْسٌ	عِلْمٍ
جً=جَنْ	مٌ=مُنْ	قَمَرٌ	شَكُوْرٌ
إٍ = إِنْ	رًا = رَنْ	عُمْيٌ	طَيْرًا
بٍ=بِنْ	بَدْرٍ	بَاسِطٌ	قَرِيْبٌ
جٍ=جِنْ	قَدْرٍ	سَمِيْعٌ	نُسُكٍ
أٌ = أُنْ	نَفْسٍ	عَلِيْمٌ	جَهْرَةً
بٌ=بُنْ	بَعْضٍ	رِزْقًا	قُرَيْشٍ
جٌ=جُنْ	شَأْنٍ	عُسْرًا	عِنَبًا
ةً = تَنْ	شَيْءٍ	يَدًا	أَنْعَمْتَ

ةٍ = تِنْ	نَاصِرٍ	هُدًى	مِنْهُمْ
ةٌ = تُنْ	دَارٌ	قُدْرَةً	صِنْوَانٌ
بُنْيَانٌ	فَرَقْنَا	أَنْشَرَ	قَادِرٍ
مِنْ أَجَلٍ	تَبْتَغِيْ	أُنْزِلَ	قَوْلاً غَيْرَ
وَانْحَرْ	غِشَاوَةٌ	بِئْرٌ	يَتِيْمًا
مِنْ خَوْفٍ	نُوْحِيْهِ	تَحْيَوْنَ	ذَا مَقْرَبَةٍ
نَارٌ حَامِيَةٌ	فَوْقَهَا	تَأْوِيْلُ	أَعْلَمُ
يَنْقَلِبُ	عَلَيْهِمْ	رُءُوْسُك	مَا تُبْدُوْن
عَيْنٌ جَارِيَةٌ	أَنْتَ	يُسْرًا	بَعِيْدًا
الْحَمْدُ	عِنْدَ	رَءُوْفٌ	مَصِيْرًا

Lesson 9

Erect *Faṭḥah* (ـٰ=ā) pronounces like Alif *Maddah*, Erect *Kasrah* (ـٖ=ī) pronounces like *Yaa Maddah*. — And Inverted *Ḍammah* (ـٗ=ū)pronounces like Waaw *Maddah*.

Nā	نٰ = نَا	Āa	ءٰ = أَا
Yā	يٰ = يَا	Bā	بٰ = بَا
Īe	ءٖ = إِيْ	Jā	جٰ = جَا
Bī	بٖ = بِيْ	Dā	دٰ = دَا
Jī	جٖ = جِيْ	ص Ṣā	صٰ = صَا
Dī	دٖ = دِيْ	ط Ṭā	طٰ = طَا
Sī	سٖ = سِيْ	Fā	فٰ = فَا
ض Ḍī	ضٖ = ضِيْ	ع Āa	عٰ = عَا
ظ Ẓī	ظٖ = ظِيْ	Lā	لٰ = لَا

Ghī	غِ = غِـيْ	Mā	مَ = مَـا
Zū	زُ = زُوْ	Qī	قِ = قِـيْ
Rū	رُ = رُوْ	Kī	كِ = كِـيْ
Shū	شُ = شُـوْ	Wī	وِ = وِيْ
Fū	فُ = فُـوْ	Hī	هِـ = هِـيْ
Lū	لُ = لُـوْ	Ủoo	ءُ = أُوْ
Mū	مُ = مُـوْ	Bū	بُ = بُـوْ
Wū	وُ = وُوْ	Jū	جُ = جُوْ
Hū	هُـ = هُـوْ	Khū	خُ = خُـوْ

Some more Words

Ma-tā	مَتٰى	Aā-da-ma	اٰدَمَ
Ka-fā	كَفٰى	Aā-ma-na	اٰمَنَ
Yaḥ-yā	يَحْيٰى	Qā-la	قٰلَ
Sul-ṭā-nun	سُلْطٰنٌ	Qā-la	قَالَ
Ī-lā-ha	إِلٰهَ	Mā-li-ki	مَالِكِ
Ma-āā-ri-bu	مَآرِبُ	Mā-li-ki	مٰلِكِ
Ha-wā-hu	هَوٰهُ	Hā-dhā	هٰذَا
Ya-rā-hu	يَرٰهُ	Dhā-li-ka	ذٰلِكَ
Ta-rā-ka	تَرٰكَ	Bi-hī	بِهٖ
Ta-la-hā	تَلٰهَا	Fī-hī	فِيْهِ
Sa-mā-wā-tin	سَمٰوٰتٍ	Nū-ri-hī	نُوْرِهٖ
Aā-ya-ti-nā	اٰيٰتِنَا	Ba-di-hī	بَعْدِهٖ

Ka-li-mā-ti-hī	كَلِمٰتِهٖ	Qab-li-hī	قَبْلِهٖ
Sub-ḥā-na-hū	سُبْحٰنَهٗ	Qī-li-hī	قِيْلِهٖ
Ib-rā-hī-ma	إِبْرَاهٖمَ	Ru-su-li-hī	رُسُلِهٖ
Iē-lā-fi-him	إِلٰفِهِمْ	Ṣifā-ti-hī	صِفَاتِهٖ
Yuḥ-yī	يُحْيٖ	La-hū	لَهٗ
Yas-ta-woo-na	يَسْتَوٗنَ	Ya-ra-hū	يَرَهٗ
Naḥ-nū	نَحْنُ	Ma-aa-hū	مَعَهٗ
La-hū	لَهٗ	Sa-mi-aa-hū	سَمِعَهٗ
Mus-li-mū-na	مُسْلِمُوْنَ	Ḥaw-la-hū	حَوْلَهٗ
Is-ḥā-qa	إِسْحٰقَ	An-za-la-hū	أَنْزَلَهٗ
Is-mā-iē-la	إِسْمٰعِيْلَ	In-da-hū	عِنْدَهٗ
Da-wū-da	دَاوٗدَ	Yan-ṣu-ru-hū	يَنْصُرُهٗ

Exercise 9

سٗ = سُوْ	قٖ = قِيْ	كٰ = كَا	ءٰ = اٰ
شٗ = شُوْ	لٖ = لِيْ	مٰ = مَا	بٰ = بَا
صٗ = صُوْ	نٖ = نِيْ	وٰ = وَا	جٰ = جَا
طٗ = طُوْ	مٖ = مِيْ	يٰ = يَا	حٰ = حَا
غٗ = غُوْ	وٖ = وِيْ	ءٖ = إِيْ	دٰ = دَا
قٗ = قُوْ	هٖ = هِيْ	بٖ = بِيْ	رٰ = رَا
كٗ = كُوْ	يٖ = يِيْ	تٖ = تِيْ	زٰ = زَا
مٗ = مُوْ	يٖ = يِيْ	خٖ = خِيْ	سٰ = سَا
نٗ = نُوْ	ءٗ = أُوْ	ذٖ = ذِيْ	صٰ = صَا
وٗ = وُوْ	بٗ = بُوْ	شٖ = شِيْ	طٰ = طَا
هٗ = هُوْ	جٗ = جُوْ	ضٖ = ضِيْ	عٰ = عَا
يٗ = يُوْ	رٗ = رُوْ	ظٖ = ظِيْ	فٰ = فَا

قَالَ = قٰلَ	اٰمَنَ	نُوْرِهٖ	سَبِيْلِهٖ
سُبْحَانَكَ	بِهٖ	بَعْدِهٖ	مَالِهٖ
سُبْحٰنَكَ	فِيْهِ	قَبْلِهٖ	كُتُبِهٖ
كَلِمَاتٍ	يُ حْ يٖ	قِيْلِهٖ	لَ هُ وْ
كَلِمٰتٍ	يُحْيٖ	رُسُلِهٖ	لَهُوْ
قٰنِتٰتٍ	إِبْرٰهٖمَ	صِفَاتِهٖ	لَهٗ
اٰدَمَ	نُوْرِهٖ يْ	وَجْهِهٖ	أَمْرُهٗ

مَالِكِ = مٰلِكِ	ذَالِكَ = ذٰلِكَ
كِتَابُ = كِتٰبُ	بِمُزَحْزِحِهٖ

دَاوُوْدَ	حَمِدَهٗ	سُلْطٰنَهٗ
دَاوٗدَ	أَخْرَجَهٗ	مَوَازِنُهٗ
كَلِمٰتُهٗ	سُبْحٰنَهٗ	مَوَازِيْنُهٗ
أَثْقَلَهٗ	سُلْطَانَهٗ	عِنْدَهٗ

يَــرَهٗ	رَازِقِيْــنَ	جِئْنٰهُمْ
يَنْصُرُهٗ	غُفْرَانَكَ	وَأْتُوْنِيْ
عَرْشَــهٗ	يَسْـَٔمُوْنَ	تَلْــوٗنَ
أَخْلَدَهٗ	أَبَــوَيْــهِ	بِالْــهُدٰي
نَــحْنُ لَــهٗ	قَرَأْتَ	إِسْمٰعِــيْلَ
مُسْلِمُوْنَ	فَاكِهَةٍ	وَإِسْحٰقَ
تَكَــاثُــرُ	اٰذَانِــهِمْ	وَيَعْقُــوْبَ
عَــلَيْنَا	مِكٰــلَ	وَلَاتَعْثَــوْا
تَرَوْنَــهُمْ	صَلٰوةٌ	فِي الْأَرْضِ
حِسَابِيَهْ	وُسْعَهَــا	مُفْسِدِيْنَ
شَهَادَةً	تُرْزَقٰنِهٖ	تَعْلَمُوْنَ
لِلْخُرُوْجِ	تُرْزَقَانِهٖ	تُجْــزَوْنَ

Lesson 10

(Jab-ba = جَ بَّ) (Dab-ba = دَبَّ)

This sign (ـــّـ) written above the Arabic alphabet is called "*Shaddah*". The alphabet with "*Shaddah*" is joined with the former alphabet and will be pronounced twice like the letter "s" in 'dis-solve'.

Bus-su	بُسُّ	**Áb-ba**	أَبْ بَ = أَبَّ
Ṣaf-fa	صَفَّ	**Án-na**	أَنْ نَ = أَنَّ
Ṣif-fi	صِفِّ	**Áj-ja**	أَجْ جَ = أَجَّ
Ṣuf-fu	صُفُّ	**Bas-sa**	بَ سْ سَ = بَسَّ
Áb-ban	أَبًّا	**Rub-ba**	رُبْ بَ = رُبَّ
Áb-bin	أَبٍّ	**Úf-fin**	أُفْ فٍ = أُ فٍّ
Áb-bun	أَبٌّ	**Ím-ma**	إِمْ مَ = إِمَّ
Íj-jan	إِجًّا	**Bas-sa**	بَسَّ
Íj-jin	إِجٍّ	**Bis-si**	بِسِّ

Thum-ma	ثُــمَّ	Ủj-jun	أُجٌّ
Sakh-khara	سَخَّرَ	Ṣuf-fan	صُفًّا
Qud-dira	قُدِّرَ	Ṣuf-fin	صُفٍّ
Tab-bat	تَبَّــتْ	Ṣuf-fun	صُفٌّ

Some more words

Ảy-yoo-ba	أَيُّــوْبَ	Rab-bī	رَبِّــيْ
Kuw-wi-rat	كُوِّرَتْ	Ịn-nī	إِنِّــيْ
Lis-sil-mi	لِلسِّلْمِ	Ảl-la-ma	عَلَّــمَ
Al-lā	اَلّٰ	Ḥat-tā	حَتّــٰى
Wal-lā	وَالّٰ	Kal-lā	كَــلَّا
Al-lā-hu	اللّٰهُ	Rab-ba-nā	رَبَّــنَا
Wal-lā-hu	وَاللّٰهُ	Ịy-yāka	إِيَّــاكَ
Ad-dun-yā	الدُّنْيَــا	Ghaf-fā-ru	غَفَّــارُ

Wan-nas-la	وَالنَّسْلَ	Sij-jee-lin	سِجِّيلٍ
Al-Qur-āna	الْقُرْاٰنَ	Fasab-biḥ	فَسَبِّحْ
Lidh-dhik-ri	لِلذِّكْرِ	Rab-bi-him	رَبِّهِمْ

Walā-kin-na	وَلٰكِنَّ
Ákh-khar-ta-nī	أَخَّرْتَنِي
Ṣar-raf-nā	صَرَّفْنَا
Fa-úm-mu-hū	فَأُمُّهُ
Nab-biá-hum	نَبِّئْهُمْ
Yadh-dhak-kara	يَذَّكَّرَ
Wa-laqal-yas-sar-nā	وَلَقَدْ يَسَّرْنَا
Ad-dun-yā	الدُّنْيَا

Exercise 10

أَبْ بَ = أَبَّ	أَنْ نَ = أَنَّ
أَجْ جَ = أَجَّ	بَ سْ سَ = بَسَّ

أَبَّ	صُفُّ	صُفُّ	كَـــلَّا
إِجَّ	بُسُّ	ثُـــمَّ	رَبَّنَـــا
صَفَّ	أَبَّـــا	سَـــخَّرَ	إِيَّـــاكَ
بُسَّ	أَبِّ	قُـــدِّرَ	غَفَّـــارُ
إِبِّ	أَبُّ	تَبَّتْ	سِجِّيلٍ
إِجِّ	إِجًّا	حُقَّتْ	فَسَبِّحْ
صَفَّ	إِجِّ	رَبِّـــيْ	رَبِّـــهِمْ
بِسِّ	إِجُّ	إِنِّـــيْ	أَيُّـــوْبَ

أُبُّ	صُفٍّ	عَلَّمَ	وَلٰكِنَّ
أُجُّ	اَلّ	حَتّى	أَخَّرْتَنِي
كُوِّرَتْ	وَالّ	وَالنَّسْلَ	لِلذِّكْرِ
صَرَّفْنَا	اللّٰهُ	نَبِّئْهُمْ	عَرَبِيٌّ
فَأُمُّهُ	وَاللّٰهُ	يَذَّكَّرَ	مُحَمَّدٌ
لِلسِّلْمِ	الدُّنْيَا	وَلَقَدْ	مُسَلَّمَةٌ
صُفًّا	يَسَّرْنَا الْقُرْاٰنَ		لِلذِّكْرِ

Lesson 11

The Arabic alphabet with mark (*Maddah* ~) will be prolonged three or four times.

(Māaa = مــآ) (Māa = مــآ)

Aalāa	عَلَــىٰ	Mā	مَــا
Māaa-áa	مَــآءَ	Māa	مــآ
Dāaa-án	دَآءً	Māaa	مَــآ
Ṣāaa-in	صَآءٍ	Lā	لَا
Ba-lāaa-ún	بَلَآءٌ	Lāa	لَآ
Ināa	إِنَّــآ	Lāaa	لَآ
Ḍooo-ú	ضُــوْٓءُ	Fiii	فِــيْٓ
Wa-ri-tha-hū		وَرِثَــهٗٓ	
Āaal-áa-na		آلْــئٰنَ	

Fii-áw-lā-di-kum	فِـــيْ أَوْلَادِكُـــمْ
Ú-lāāa-íka-hum	أُولَٰٓئِـــكَ هُـــمْ
Bimāa-ún-zi-la	بِـــمَـــآ أُنْــزِلَ
Banii-Ís-rāāa-íeela	بَنِـــيْٓ إِسْـــرَآءِ يْلَ
Ịdhā-jāāa-āa	إِذَا جَـــآءَ
Naṣ-rul-lā-hi	نَصْـــرُ اللهِ
Íl-lāa-án-fu-sa-hum	إِلَّآ أَنْفُسَـــهُمْ
Fa-man-ḥāāaj-ja-ka	فَـــمَنْ حَـــآجَّكَ

Exercise 11

مَـــا	لَآ	مَـــآءَ	إِنَّـــآ
مَـــآ	لَآ	دَآءً	ضُـــوٓءُ
مَـــآ	فِـــيٓ	صَـــآءٍ	وَرِثَـــهُۥٓ
لَا	عَـــلَىٓ	بَلَآءٌ	ءَآلْـــٔـنَ

فِـــيٓ أَوْلَادِكُـــمْ	إِذَا جَآءَ نَصْرُ ٱللَّهِ
أُولَٰٓئِـــكَ هُـــمْ	إِلَّآ أَنْفُسَهُـــمْ
بِـــمَآ أُنْـــزِلَ إِلَيْكَ	فَمَـــنْ حَـــآجَّكَ
بَـــنِيٓ إِسْرَٰٓءِيـــلَ	إِلَّا مَـــا شَآءَ ٱللَّهُ

Lesson 12

The alphabet in "*Muqaṭ-ṭiaāt*" Words are pronounced separately.

Ḥā-Meeem	حٰمٓ	**Nooon**	نٓ
Yā-Seeen	يٰسٓ	**Qaaaf**	قٓ
Ṭā-Hā	طٰهٰ	**Ṣaaad**	صٓ

Aeeen-Seeen Qaaaf	عٓسٓقٓ
Alif-Laaam-Rā	الٓر
Ṭā-Seeen	طٰسٓ
Ṭā-Seeen - Meeem	طٰسٓمٓ
Alif-Laaam-Meeem	الٓمٓ
Alif-Laaam-Meeem Rā	الٓمٓر
Kaaaf-Hā-Yā-Aeeen-Ṣaaad	كٓهيعٓصٓ
Alif-Laaam-Meeem-Ṣaaad	الٓمٓصٓ

Exercise 12

نٓ	الٓرٰ
قٓ	طسٓ
صٓ	طسٓمٓ
حمٓ	الٓمٓ
يسٓ	الٓمٓرٰ
طه	كٓهيعٓصٓ
عٓسٓقٓ	الٓمٓصٓ

Lesson 13

The alphabet with "*Sukoon*" (ـْـ) is omitted before the alphabet with "*Shaddah*" (ـّـ)like. (Ím-ma = إِنْ مَّا)

Miw-wa	مِنْ وَّ	Lad-da	لَتْ دَّ
Siw-wa	سِ وَّ	Qat-ta	قَدْ تَّ
Dhal-la	ذً لَّ	Luk-ku	لُقْكُّ
In-nun	ءٍ نٌّ	Al-la	اَ نْ لَّ
Jum-mu	جٌ مٌّ	Ám-ma	عَنْ مَّ
Bay-ya	بً يَّ	Daw-wa	دً وَّ
Án-dā-daw-wa-án-tum	أَنْدَادًا وَّأَنْتُـــمْ		
Miw-wa-raaa-i-him	مِنْ وَّرَآئِــهِـــمْ		

ظُلُمٰتٍ لَّا يُبْصِرُوْنَ

Ẓu-lu-mā-til-lā-yub-ṣi-roon

لَنْ يَّقْدِرَ عَلَيْهِ

Lay-yaq-di-ra-ʿalay-hi

إِنَّ اللّٰهَ غَفُوْرٌ رَّحِيْمٌ

Ín-nal-lā-ha-gha-fū-rur-ra-ḥeemun

Exercise 13

لَتْ دَّ = لَــدَّ	اَنْ لَّ = اَلَّ	مٌ وَّ = مُــنْوَّ
قَدْتَّ = قَتَّ	عَنْ مَّ = عَــمَّ	مٌ يَّ = مُنْــيَّ
إِنْ مَّ = إِمَّ	جٌ مُّ = جُــمُّ	أَنْ لَّآ إِلٰــهَ
لُقْكُّ = لُكُّ	مِــنْ وَّ = مِنْوَّ	مِنَ السَّمَــآءِ
دَوَّ = دَنْــوَّ	سٍ وَّ = سِنْوَّ	مِنْ رَّبِّــكَ

نَصْرٌ مِّنَ اللّٰهِ	مِــنْ لَّدُنْــهُ
أَنْدَادًا وَ أَنْتُــمْ	مِــنْ وَّرَآئِــهِمْ
ظُلُمٰتِ لَّا يُبْصِــرُوْنَ	لَنْ يَّقْدِرَ عَلَيْــهِ
اِرْكَبْ مَّعَنَــا	مَــرْقُوْمٌ يَّشْهَدُ
مَــنْ يُّــؤْمِــنُ	إِنَّ اللّٰهَ غَفُوْرٌ رَّحِيْمٌ

Lesson 14

(i) If Noon with *Sukoon* or *Tanween* comes before "Baa" then it is pronounced "Meem".

Ra-sū-lum-bimā	رَسُوْلٌۢ بِمَا
Ám-ba-á-hum	أَنْبَأَهُمْ
Mim-baʿa-di-hī	مِنْۢ بَعْدِهٖ
Kha-bī-ram-ba-ṣī-ran	خَبِيْرًاۢ بَصِيْرًا
Naf-sum-bi-mā	نَفْسٌۢ بِمَا
Sum-bu-lā-tin	سُنۢبُلٰتٍ
Raj-ʿum-ba-ʿiee-dun	رَجْعٌۢ بَعِيْدٌ
ʿAlee-mum-bi-mā	عَلِيْمٌۢ بِمَا
Fa-nā-ẓi-ra-tum-bi-ma	فَنٰظِرَةٌۢ بِمَ

(ii) The small alphabet "Noon" (ن) in between two alphabets is joint with the alphabet coming next to Noon. It is called "*Noon Quṭni*" and will be pronounced with "*Kasrah*" (ـِ).

Nū-ḥu-nib-na-hū	نُــوْحُ نِ ابْنَــهُ
Qa-dī-ru-nil-la-dhee	قَــدِيْرُ نِ الَّذِيْ
Ma-tha-la-nil-qaw-mi	مَثَــلاً نِ الْقَــوْمِ
Khay-ra-nil-wa-ṣiy-ya-tu	خَيْرَ نِ الْوَصِيَّةُ
Yaw-ma-i-dhi-nil-masā-qu	يَوْمَئِذِ نِ الْمَسَاقُ
Shay-á-nit-ta-khadha	شَيْئًا نِ اتَّــخَــذَ

Exercise 14

رَسُوْلٌ بِمَا	عَلِيْمٌ بِمَا
مِنْ بَعْدِهٖ	نُوْحُ نِ ابْنَهٗ
أَنْبَأَهُمْ	قَدِيْرُ نِ الَّذِيْ
خَبِيْرًا بَصِيْرًا	خَيْرَ نِ الْوَصِيَّةُ
سُنْبُلٰتٍ	مَثَلَا نِ الْقَوْمِ
نَفْسٌ بِمَا	يَوْمَئِذِ نِ الْمَسَاقُ
رَجْعٌ بَعِيْدٌ	شَيْئَا نِ اتَّخَذَ

Lesson 15

(i) When one stops at Round Taa (ة), it will Pronounced like "Haa".

Quw-wa-tan	قُوَّةً ط
Quw-wah	قُوَّهْ
Al-qā-ri-ʿaa-tu	الْقَارِعَةُ ○
Alqā-ri-ʿaah	الْقَارِعَهْ
Ka-li-ma-tan	كَلِمَةً ج
Ka-li-mah	كَلِمَهْ
Shir-ʿaa-tan	شِرْعَةً ز
Shir-ʿaah	شِرْعَهْ
Kha-lee-fa-tan	خَلِيْفَةً م
Kha-lee-fah	خَلِيْفَهْ

(ii) The small alphabet "Seen" (ۜ) is written above " ص = Ṣaad" as (صۜ), this "Ṣ̃aad" can be read as Seen or Ṣ̃aad both.

Yab-su-ṭu	يَبْصُۜطُ
Bas-ṭa-tan	بَصْۜطَةً
Bi-mu-s̃ay-ṭi-rin	بِمُصَۜيْطِرٍ
Hu-mul-mu-s̃ay-ṭi-roona	هُمُ الْمُصَۜيْطِرُوْنَ

Exercise 15

قُوَّةً ط قُوَّهْ	وَيَبْصُۜطُ
الْقَارِعَةُ ○ الْقَارِعَهْ	بَصْۜطَةً
كَلِمَةً ج كَلِمَهْ	بِمُصَۜيْطِرٍ
شِرْعَةً ز شِرْعَهْ	هُمُ الْمُصَۜيْطِرُوْنَ
خَلِيْفَةً خَلِيْفَهْ	

DARUSSALAM
GLOBAL LEADER IN ISLAMIC BOOKS
Riyadh · Jeddah · Al-Khobar · Sharjah
Lahore · London · Houston · New York